Thank you for buy[ing]
I hope you enjo[y]

I CAN HEAR YOU IRONING

Poems on Comparison Culture, Imperfect Parenting,
and Why Social Media Is Largely Nonsense

Kate Hook

First published 2024

Copyright © Kate Hook
Cover design and illustrations © Paul Loudon

Published under license by Brown Dog Books and The Self-Publishing Partnership Ltd, 10b Greenway Farm, Bath Rd, Wick, nr. Bath BS30 9RL

www.selfpublishingpartnership.co.uk

ISBN printed book: 978-1-83952-764-7

ISBN e-book: 978-1-83952-765-4

Printed and bound by CPI Group (UK) Ltd, Croydon, CR0 4YY

This book is printed on FSC© certified paper

MIX
Paper | Supporting
responsible forestry
FSC
www.fsc.org
FSC® C013604

This book is dedicated to my big sister Marie -
the most badass of all the badass bitches I've ever met,
and believe me, I've met a few!

About the Author

Kate is a lactose-intolerant cheese fetishist who was born in Wythenshawe, a council estate in South Manchester. She now lives in Sale (primarily because they have a better selection of cheeses) with her husband and two children.

Kate has been writing poetry since she was about six or seven years old, which was also the period that she used to binge-watch *Home & Away* and pretend to be Australian. It is also when she was secretly in love with Timmy Mallett... thank heavens that neither of these events inspired any early poems!

She describes herself as a "fair weather feminist" because putting out bins is arguably her husband's job, but she'll happily fight to close the gender pay gap, or end violence against women any day of the week.

Much of Kate's poetry has a ruthless rummage into the unrealistic expectations that modern society places on people (mainly women!) and why we need to just step away from the bullshit.

About the Illustrator

Paul is a freelance illustrator and graphic artist based in Stretford, Manchester. He spends more time in his shed than his wife and children would possibly like, but that's where all the magic is created!

Employing a traditional comic book style in his artwork, Paul's diverse talents have been used for video game artwork, storyboarding, children's books, and to create the cover art for cult TV and film magazine *Starburst*. He's also a firm favourite with the BBC, having done commissions for BBC Online, BBC Sport and CBeebies across various projects.

When he's not sketching away in his shed, Paul can be found running around the streets of Stretford and Chorlton or adding honey to his coffee instead of sugar.

You can check out his fabulous work on **paulloudon.com** or **@loudon.illustrator** on Instagram.

TABLE OF CONTENTS

Chapter One: I Can Hear You Ironing

Hurrah for Imperfect Parenting

When my first son was born, I struggled a lot with what I now realise was post-natal depression. In desperation I took to social media for reassurance that these feelings were normal, and instead I came across a vast landscape of Insta-perfect new mums in pastel-coloured pyjamas saying they were #blessed and #cherishingeverysecond which did nothing to help me feel that I was normal.

Once I gained the confidence to venture out, I seemed to get inundated with incredibly intrusive, unsolicited advice from complete strangers. Disappointingly it was often other women (mainly older women) who did not do this in a kind way, but instead scolded me for not dressing my son in enough layers or told me I was irresponsible for taking my baby swimming when he was a few weeks old.

Then once you throw in society's ten pence worth that mums should go back to work.... but somehow magically stay home and raise our children too, then we just can't win, can we?

It's high time everyone wound their necks in and trusted women to make whichever choices are right for their families!

Cherish Every Moment

"Cherish every moment, because they're not this small for long!"
Thank fuck I think, then shrink with shame, as I feel all kinds of wrong.
"You won't get this time back" I'm warned, by a stranger in the park.
I'm fully aware of the chronological nature of time I want to bark!

But instead, I slap on my "mummy smile" - the one I've used lots already today.
"Oh, I know. It goes so quick!" I gush!
That's what mums are supposed to say.

Should I cherish each night wake up? Or a sofa streaked with poo?
"You're lucky – some folk can't have kids. Just be thankful that you do!"

Should I cherish wiping the streams of snot that come with each cold and cough?
"Well, I went back to work after just six weeks, had no option to just stay off!"

Should I cherish being late for school pick up? Nearly died in the dash to get here!
"Well, you can't have it all. Besides, what do you expect when you selfishly chose your career?"

So, I've decided to cherish some moments.
You're right! Cherishing's making me happy!
But they don't involve scraping dried beans off the floor or changing a nuclear nappy.

No, I'm cherishing wine after bedtime, or a blackberry gin over ice.
I'm cherishing the knowledge I simply can't win, even with every fucker's "advice."

I'm cherishing blocking out ALL the noise, and I don't just mean noise from my kids.
But from perma-affronted, dusty-cunted, Daily-Mail reading old bids!

I've abandoned all plans to be perfect, in a culture where everything I do.
Will always be judged, criticized, or compared – and I'd urge you to do the same too!

So, mums – raise your glass. Let's say FUCK IT and pour!
Let's toast imperfection with gin.
Cherish every moment? Fuck THAT
Let's cherish ourselves for the win!

There's a reason that sleep deprivation is used as a form of torture, and any new parent will understand the sheer desperation surrounding this. I wrote this poem whilst thinking back to how utterly mental I was during the first few months of having a newborn, and the ridiculous insults and accusations that I would spit at my husband as we passed on the landing at 5am to "swap shifts" and look after the baby.

One day I accused him of sneaking off to iron his work clothes as a way of shirking his fatherhood duties, which is something we now laugh about. Kind of...

I Can Hear You Ironing

It's 5am, how much sleep did I get?
Two hours perhaps? Maybe three?
Surely this child can't have woken again?
Can he hear that? Or is it just me?

"I'm tired" he declares and throws in a yawn,
This type of scene too commonplace
I picture taking the breastfeeding pillow,
and holding it over his face.

"Please will you take him?" I humbly beg.
"He can lie in the bath while you shower."
"He likes watching his dad getting ready for work
 and it means I could grab one more hour!"

What d'ya mean "not today?" Why the bloody hell not?
You've an 8am meeting? WHO CARES?!
He sensibly flees from the war zone
as more missiles are hurled down the stairs.

"I can hear you ironing!" I text from the next room,
as irrational rage slowly climbs.
A small hungry mouth chomps away at my breast
as I mentally compile his crimes.

I once flashed SOS with the bedside lamp,
hoping someone would answer my plea.
But at just 4am, the rescue boat was asleep.
I'm well and truly lost at sea.

This poem is for anyone who questions every bit of their moral fibre when they order off Amazon. But when you've got kids, and those kids are little, it's just so bloody convenient isn't it?

I'm possibly going to hell, but as long as it has Prime then I can order a fan to cool me down....

Amazon

OK, yes – very questionable human rights,
But sometimes in life, you need moss-green tights,
For your child, who's a sprite in his Christmas play
And you've only just been advised today
of the wardrobe needs of this critical role
So, you click. And you scroll. And it murders your soul.
But you hit *add to basket* nonetheless,
and berate yourself for being a chaotic hot mess:
who will now be sat up for the rest of the night,
searching *boy's fairy costumes* to kit out your sprite.
And yes, you could go out, and source some tights BUT
it's now quarter to midnight, and Asda is shut.
And with free next day delivery – come on – who could want more?
Oh Jeff, your sinful offerings are hard to ignore.

Now you're watching the play,
and you're bursting with pride,
and you're hoping that no migrant workers have died,
In this last-minute quest to ship green tights to you
and your child, who's been cast as *Sprite #2.*

In November 2020, as if going through a pandemic wasn't shitty enough, we lost a pregnancy at eight weeks. Trying to navigate the whole medical process amid Covid was a minefield – nobody seemed to know what to do with me or where to send me, but I seemed to end up in the Early Pregnancy Unit quite a bit.

The Early Pregnancy Unit (or EPU) is where pregnant women are sent before they've reached the "holy grail" of twelve weeks pregnancy. In that room there was a mixture of women who were attending check-ups after bleeding, women who already knew they'd lost their pregnancies, and women who were actively in the process of miscarrying their babies.

In the middle of the room was a little tree, strewn with paper stars. It was in the centre of the room so there was no way you could avoid looking at it. The stars were messages written by grieving parents to all their babies who never made it earthside.

I hoped and prayed (I'm not religious so I don't know who I prayed to!) that I wouldn't be one of those writing a message…

Paper Stars

I stare at each branch for far too long.
Words of love etched on a star
A note for each life that the world wouldn't honour
I'm hoping that's not what you are.

Just here for a scan, and I'm sure it's all fine
I'll be out of here in a while
Clutching monochrome grainy pictures
Disguising my soppy smile.

I'll avoid all eye contact with others
Occupants of each hard plastic chair
With their solemn sad faces, they wait for their turn
But they already know why they're there.

The gel is a glacial rip tide
Watch me drown, under feelings of love
Just swirling around as I stare at the sky
Where the sun's just a strip light above.

Now the water is still, and I'm listening
For that one sound I desperately crave
But I know that I'm under the ocean
And the silence hits rocks like a wave

I could write you a message on paper stars
And you'd live there forever, on that tree
But what could I say that would make any sense?
When you never got the chance to be?

I'm sure I don't have to give too much detail to explain where or when I wrote this one...

A Spectator Sport

I can't see a child, but I know that one's there.
The tell-tale sign is a creaking stair.
In a minute, as has happened oft times before,
The head of that child will peep round the door.

And with the door then flung open, and the bathroom raided,
My right to privacy has been invaded.
I've tried to lock it, to keep the child out,
but he tends to just stand on the landing and shout...

"Mummy! Mummy! I can't tie my shoes!"
(Note he's walked PAST his father, to give me this news)
Or "Henry's just drawn on my new reading book!"
Or sometimes just "Look, mummy, mummy, mummy LOOK!"

Whatever happened to women's rights?
Is a girl not entitled to some private shites?
I bellow the words, all angered and fraught...
"This is NOT a spectator sport!"

Just five bloody minutes is all that I ask.
I'm not fleeing the country to go and bask
By Aegean seas, in sun-soaked Greece!
I just want to have a poo in peace!

Interesting fact. It takes the same amount of time to read this poem as it takes my husband to say something infuriating and ridiculous…

Separate Bedrooms

"Nice of them to give us a lie in" he grins,
Appearing all fresh at the door.

Nice of them to give YOU one, I think.
They've been in bed with me since half four!

I recently saw a debate play out on social media about parent child parking spaces and was amazed at how there was so much resentment (from the older generation in particular) about these spaces. Everyone seemed to miss the point that the spaces were there to make people's lives that little bit easier... nobody wants a child to bolt across a car park, or get a dent in their door from someone trying to wrestle a car seat out!

What I observed from the discussion is that previous generations seem really upset by a lot of things that we'd now call "progress" in our society. This really baffled me, because why wouldn't you want your children and grandchildren to have things easier?!

The main argument was that these things weren't available in their day, so how very dare we expect to hope for brighter futures...

In My Day

Parent child parking? We never had that in my day.
We just cracked on; we made no fuss.
We had no car; I got the bus.
All these privileges you have are a massive plus,
and I never had that in my day.

Your day was 1964
Where the average car was not five-door
You never dared to hope for more.
That's why you never had it in your day.

14

Autism? We never had that in my day.
It's proper parenting they lack.
Kids never dared to answer back.
You misbehaved; you got a smack.
No, we never had that in my day.

Ah, you mean the days when it was cool
To physically punish kids in school?
Use slurs like retard, dunce, and fool?
That's what it was like in your day.

Maternity rights? We never had those in my day.
We knew to just accept the fact
that we got pregnant, we got sacked.
Maternity Discrimination Act?
No, we never had that in our day.

And you really think it was OK
that a woman who was in the family way
was deprived of her human rights, and pay?
I bet you wish you'd had it in your day.

#MeToo? We never had all that in my day.
A whistle in the street? We simply smiled.
It never made us anxious or riled.
Whistle now at a lass and complaints get filed.
No, we never had that in my day.

Call me fussy, but I like to walk down the street.
Without being treated like a piece of meat
Or fearing the sound of too-near feet
You really should have started that in your day.

When trying to get back into work after maternity leave, I started to feel a little awkward about the gap in my CV. A gap that I'd spent doing some pretty hardcore parenting, and NOT sitting around eating cake as I think some potential employers assumed. I started to think about how working parents are one of the most valuable assets that a company can have – nobody is better at getting shit done than a parent who has a looming nursery pick up, and nobody is better at multi-tasking!

I started to think about all the stuff that a parent must do (often on top of working!) and how these skills would be so valuable to any employer. Also, if this was an actual job advert, would anyone in their right mind even apply?!

PA Required – Immediate Start

Due to a change in circumstances
(I need some support, as the school year advances!)
I'm posting an exciting vacancy today
For a full time, live-in, household PA.

The right candidate will be patient and caring,
Must be willing to wake through the night without swearing.
Must display enthusiasm, never get tired
As administering meds in the dark is required.

You'll serve the day's meals, plus a snack before bed,
Sometimes friends come for tea, so you must plan ahead.
Some nights you'll make one meal, some nights could be three,
And the kids might refuse them, so tenacity is key.

Your organisation skills must exceed the norm,
As you'll oversee each school event, trip, and form.
You'll manage all homework, own clothes day donations,
Odd Sock Day, and Christmas play outfit creations.

40 hours per week is frequently exceeded,
And you'll have to do overtime whenever it's needed.
You can take lots of toilet breaks, but beware if you do
That small people will likely barge in while you poo!

In terms of key benefits, there's no workplace pension,
And you still have to work if you're ill, I should mention.
And the annual leave is admittedly poor,
But you *will* get a break when you drive to the store.

The successful person must be mentally sound,
Have a clean driving license to ferry kids round.
For school projects, they should hold an art degree.
Oh, and lastly, they must be willing to do ALL THIS for free.

So, if you're ambitious, hard-working, outgoing,
If you're great at project managing, nursing, and sewing,
If you can coach phonics, whilst cooking a stew
Then this might just be the career move for you!

A while back I was struggling to get my son to have breakfast before school, so I decided to invent a fun breakfast called Hippo on the Rocks – a bowl of porridge, a teaspoon of Nutella* stirred in to make the "mud" and a Kinder chocolate hippo in the middle, surrounded by the "rocks" which were blueberries and strawberries. Admittedly a bit more sugar than I would've liked, but he loved it and ate every bit, and so I reconciled it with myself that he'd at least had a decent breakfast and his brain was now fuelled and ready to learn.

Feeling all chuffed with my little self (and obviously now mentally planning the launch of my own children's cookbook!) I posted a picture of his breakfast on a Facebook page for children's recipe ideas. I thought that other parents may want to give it a try for their own little breakfast-refusers.

When I got back from the school run and checked my notifications, I had to firstly check that I hadn't accidentally uploaded a photo of a bottle of Pinot Grigio and declared that's what I'd given him for breakfast, because I couldn't believe the abuse I received for posting a picture of some chocolate porridge!

Anyway, that was my first and last post on that page, but he still eats Hippo on the Rocks each morning and is still very much alive...

Hippo on the Rocks

A chocolate hippo lounges, as the oats ooze with Nutella.
Well, what else do you expect from an artiodactyl river-dweller?
Surrounding him are blueberry "rocks" each making a sinking hole.
He knows he will be eaten soon, each scrap licked from the bowl.

A mummy watches anxiously, her child perched on a stool.
She knows he needs to eat something nutritious before school
And *of course* she would've preferred the porridge minus all the sugar.
But it's 8:15, his tie's disappeared, and he's being an awkward bugger.

A boy tucks into breakfast, oh how he loves the chocolate taste!
He's even scoffed the blueberries, not a bite will go to waste.
He pays no heed to sugar content, gives the bowl some licks.
He gives no thought to diabetes, possibly coz he's six?!

A mama scrolls a Facebook site, it's Texas where she's based,
And she's seen a post this morning that has left a bitter taste.
She's not concerned with abortion rights, or yet another gun law fail,
No – her primary concern is what a child's ate in Sale!

She taps her phone screen furiously, her cheeks aglow with rage.
"Oh man, that's child cruelty. He will not see middle age!"
But that one statement isn't enough, along comes the next bomb.
"That kid should be taken off you, you're not fit to be a mom!"

Another mama joins in, also holier-than-thou
And she is just as outraged as the first demented cow.
"Honey, THAT AIN'T BREAKFAST" she writes in a capital shout.
"Get him to a dentist before ALL HIS TEETH fall out!"

This mummy is now most confused, and completely mystified
At how a bowl of chocolate porridge is on a par with genocide.
She's really now quite anxious at the tirade of abuse.
Thank fuck she thinks *I didn't post his glass of orange juice!*

After being accused of tooth decay and neglect in one fell swoop
She finds the post, deletes it, and then leaves the fucking group.
And she can laugh about this trauma now, but to all those "perfect" mothers:
Support all mums, we're all doing our best – and don't be a dick to others!

*Other chocolate spreads are available!

21

I'm forever in awe of those wonderful writers who can bring nature and emotions to life with their words, and I don't feel like I'm one of those writers…. I'd much rather write something daft about fingering or baked beans (see later poems!)

I still don't think I can be a "proper" poet until I've written some flowery metaphors in my poetry, much like I don't think I will ever class myself as a "proper" runner no matter how much running I do. I thought I'd better give some of the flowery floaty stuff a go if I ever want to be taken seriously!

Saplings

My son brought home a sapling from school:
A Crab Apple, with a little scrawled label that clung to its plastic bag.
Nourished and grown in the school gardens,
and given the same tender love and care that's usually reserved for our children.

I cried a little when I held it,
as it was no different from my other little sapling;
The one holding out the plastic bag in his ink-stained hands,
eager to tell me some facts he'd learned today about roots, and how trees drink water.

I thought how that sapling would soon grow.
How I would give it nourishment that would feed its strength
And how one day I would look and say *Hey, when did you get so big?!*
And I'd remember how tiny and vulnerable that sapling was on that first day
When we took it home, and nobody was quite sure what to do next.

But mainly I cried because I thought "Great, something else I have to try and keep alive!"

During a spell of insanity last year, I agreed to be the parent representative for my son's year group. I thought with my work background in communications that this would be a piece of piss, but I was NOT prepared for this role whatsoever, namely a lot of the messages that used to pop up on a daily (and nightly) basis. I'm sure that any parent on a school WhatsApp group will relate…

The School WhatsApp Group

Hi everyone, can I just make sure,
PE this week – indoor? Outdoor?
Do they just need shorts? Or sweaters? Or more?
Are they likely to go on wet grass?

Hi guys, for forest school, who's wearing what?
Oh, is that today? I'd completely forgot!
Is it waterproofs, wellies and hats? Or not?
Can they store their kit bags in class?

Can anyone tell me, if you happen to know?
Is this the week that the kids all go
To the library – but is it on? Even though
They'll be dressed up for World Book Day?

Well Orla's in wellies, but with shoes in her bag.
I've just remembered they're new – did I take off the tag?
Hey, it's raining from 10 guys, just wanted to flag!
Oooh, I hope they're not soaked on the way!

What day does the homework need to be in?
I can't find the spellings – I've checked in the bin.
Max has coloured in the picture of Anne Boleyn,
It was a struggle to get him to do that!

Is it definitely today that reading books come home?
I could swear that the office said not when I phoned.
Sorry! Me again! For forest school, sorry to moan…
But do we know *why* the kids need a hat?

OMG guys I'm fuming, I rang Mr Bursley
Did you know there's an assembly happening on Thursday?
I can't get the time off; I'm working in Worsley!
Well, my Thomas never brought home a note!

Hun, they don't bring notes home now, it all goes online.
I believe it's this Thursday at quarter past nine.
How the hell are working parents supposed to make time?
Hey, for forest school, do the kids need a coat?

Now, you're probably thinking this shit is demented.
But this is my life, hence it needs to be vented,
I can't coat it with sugar, or make it sweet scented
And it takes up SO MUCH of my night!

I've put pre-emptive posts in attempts to dilute it.
The sensible option is probably to mute it.
At bedtime I wish I could just fucking shoot it
As when all's said and done – it's just *shite!*

The law of Christmas states: as soon as you finish your shopping, you will inevitably be asked for some rogue item that they've just decided that they might like. This year my six-year-old asked me for a phone. I said no. Largely because he's six (and who the hell would he ring? None of his mates have one!) and because I was done with my shopping and was ready to recommence my annual evening dates with cheese and Baileys.

I told him that it was too late, and that Santa has closed the list now to get ready for delivering everything. He looked at me with such searing disbelief that I knew instantly that this was quite possibly the last year I'd have a believer – and it hurt my very fragile mummy heart!

Dinosaur Cake

I reluctantly wrap up Christmas gifts.
Red paper – Paw Patrol
I'm pondering time and how it shifts;
It's evaded my keen control.

I Sellotape up a bulky box
He's saved for a Smart TV
He's been earning money, pairing socks,
And drying dishes after tea.

Now he'll sit and watch things in his room
And I pray for time to slow
And didn't he just come out the womb?
Where did my baby go?

At his last birthday, he was a kid,
He wanted a dinosaur cake
Yet I'm messaging "Hi, is a Netflix theme
Something that you could make?"

They grow so fast, the years dissolve,
Yet I'm clutching the same coffee cup
They scale that wall – from baby to boy.
It's us who can't catch up.

Chapter Two: I Can Hear You Scrolling

Stop Comparing Yourself on Social Media

Don't you just love it when you've had a shitty parenting day, and you start doom-scrolling on social media and see needless braggy parenting posts?

I'm not saying we shouldn't be proud of our kids or share their achievements, but I do try and hold back a bit from posting every nugget of academic merit. Largely because I'm very conscious that some people may not be having the same experience with their children for whatever reason, and the education system doesn't always suit every child. Some parents this week will be overjoyed because their child has stayed in school a whole week without having a meltdown or an anxiety attack, and for them that's their win.

Tell your child how amazing they are, how smart and clever they are, how great they are at sport... but consider whether the rest of the world always needs to know about it. If you constantly feel the need to tell the rest of the world, then ask yourself why that might be...

Little Jack

Little Jack is six years old, his mouth a gappy grin,
but absent teeth don't stop him being fluent in Mandarin.
He taught himself equations, how to sear filet mignon,
He prefers Puccini's *Madame Butterfly* to *Miss Saigon*.

Little Jack's been reading Shakespeare since the age of three.
He's bored of Biff and Chip, he says "they emanate ennui."
The curriculum doesn't challenge him, he's stagnant, bored, and sad.
He's starting Homer's *Odyssey* having read *The Iliad*.

But it's not just in the classroom where our wonder boy exceeds,
He did a fifty-mile run last week – Liverpool to Leeds!
He was signed up by Man City once they'd watched him in the park,
He could literally be a coastguard now – he once outswam a shark!

They nurture their son's talent with every pound they can afford,
And what else can us mere mortals do but sit back and applaud?
I know you want to look away, his perfection gets you riled.
But his mum needs you to know her son is BETTER THAN YOUR CHILD!

Social media can be very dark sometimes and is probably the least social thing ever! People seem to say things online that they would never dream of saying in person, and I wonder whether the safety and protection of being sat behind a screen gives them the illusion that this is OK.

I've generally found Instagram to be a much nicer place and I wonder whether the inclusion of images removes some of that dehumanisation that posting on social media can foster. Even so, we live in such an insidious "comparison culture" that I wonder whether the whole social media thing can ever really be truly healthy.

You Don't Get Twats on Instagram

Twitter (or 'X') is a dungeon for those,
Who are deeply unhappy with life – and it shows!
They'll berate news presenters for wearing bright clothes.
Fighting wars from their keyboards. So bold!

A newsreader's been cancelled, now the public want blood,
And he's tweeted a statement, won't do him much good.
Just coz you can, doesn't mean that you should.
All that Twitters is sadly not gold.

But.... You don't get twats on Instagram!

Insta's shots of people's teas,
Arty angles of artisan cheese,
Matching pyjamas and Christmas trees.
Nope – you don't get twats on Instagram!

If aliens descended on the human race
And you tried to explain the "Book of Face."
Would you call it a friendly and welcoming space?
Somewhere safe, to debate all life's issues?

Divisive misogyny spewed by The Sun
All at each other's throats, thanks to lies that they've spun.
Clarkson's cry-wanks over Meghan.... U OK hun?
Won't someone please pass him the tissues?

But.... You don't get twats on Instagram!

Inspiring quotes, not angry rants,
Set to background sounds of Buddhist chants.
Organic, vegan, fairtrade pants.
Nah – you don't get twats on Instagram!

I've played round with TikTok but it's not for me.
Probably because I'm nearly forty-three.
Don't want to watch an influencer cook his tea.
Dubbed over with a weird robot voice!

During Covid we doom-scrolled this addictive expanse
Saw prostrated paramedics do choreographed dance.
Soon the fun turned to judgement - us Brits took a stance.
"Glad to see you're so busy, boys!"

But.... You don't get twats on Instagram!

Insta proudly shares the tale.
Of how a one-time obese, miserable male
Changed his entire life - just by juicing kale!
No – you don't get twats on Instagram!

Selling temporary joy to the permanently depressed.
Telling menopausal women how they should be dressed.
Primark or Prada – which lipstick's the best?
Well, I guess it depends on the price.

The price of your sanity, the price of your soul
The price of your time as you solemnly scroll.
As you calmly compare and type HASHTAG LIFE GOAL!
Sitting pretty in fool's paradise.

But no – you don't get twats on Instagram.

I recently tried out a sound bath session with some Buddhist chanting and "singing bowls" in a bid to get some inner peace and relaxation. It seemed a good idea at the time, and all the celebs are at it, so I thought I'd give it a go.

I can safely say that it was quite possibly one of the least relaxing experiences of my entire life, and it wasn't until I came home and had a big glass of wine that I was able to fully recover from the bloody thing!

Verdict – I'm crap at enforced relaxation!

Singing Bowls

Nam Myoho Renge Kyo
I'm lying on a church hall floor.
I'm frozen to my fucking core.
Nam Myoho Renge Kyo

Nam Myoho Renge Kyo
The draft is coming from the door.
They said bring socks, I get what for
Nam Myoho Renge Kyo

Nam Myoho Renge Kyo
The chanting starts, it's loud and raw.
I try to stifle my guffaw.
Nam Myoho Renge Kyo

Nam Myoho Renge Kyo
Why can't I just unclench my jaw?
This mat is shit, my back is sore.
Nam Myoho Renge Kyo

Nam Myoho Renge Kyo
The people here are zen and pure.
They talk of peace, and ending war.
Nam Myoho Renge Kyo

Nam Myoho Renge Kyo
The chanting guy, I now abhor.
A glass of wine I want to pour.
Nam Myho Renge Kyo

Nam Myoho Renge Kyo
Some bastard has begun to snore.
This is the final fucking straw.
Nam Myoho Renge Kyo

Nam Myoho Renge Kyo
I'd give it my best shot, I swore.
But I am feeling zen no more.
Nam Myoho Renge Kyo

Bonfire Night – loved by (most) kids but if we're honest it's shit for parents, isn't it? There's usually some kind of cash-only arrangement, some muddy field to contend with for which no length of wellie boot is ever enough, and the fireworks are always later than advertised, leading to bored whiny kids. This doesn't stop everyone posting their bonfire night pictures on social media though whilst pretending they had an amazing time. But trust me – every adult hates it...

Prove me wrong!

Bang Go Expectations

Oh, is this the way they say November's meant to feel?
Or just freezing parents waiting for a Catherine Wheel?
Pulp articulate PERFECTLY just how shit this is.
All I've got to see me through is beer, no Es or wizz!

Remember, remember the fifth of November.
When your soul dies as fast as a bonfire ember
As you stand there, silently cursing your kid.
A privilege for which you've just paid fifteen quid.

Those pricey Joules wellies you hoped would come good
Are now half full of water, and rugby pitch mud
And your face turns to parchment from bonfire heat
Whilst the kids moan they're bored, and complain of wet feet.

You're wedged in a queue next to puffa-coat huns.
Just for slimy, shit hotdogs on world's driest buns
And once they're half-eaten, you withdraw your life savings,
For a weak cup of Horlicks with mint chocolate shavings.

Your own jacket stinks now – fried onions and ash.
You say no to sparklers, you've ran out of cash.
Requests for the fairground you must also refuse,
Then you mop up the meltdown that swiftly ensues.

You must leave, it's a school night, come on – it makes sense!
You all walk home bickering, everyone's tense.
Back home you're on Insta, you've opened the rum
#makingmemories #bonfirenightfun

Many poems have been written about love, in fact it's probably the most written about topic of all time. But I've not really found anything yet which sums up the love between me and my husband, as after 13 years of marriage (unlucky for some) and the daily stresses of managing kids, a mortgage, and remembering to take the bins out each Tuesday, things are probably less W.B Yeats and a bit more Yates's Wine Lodge!

So, if your relationship isn't all staring wistfully at each other and roaming hills holding hands, rest assured that's totally fine… as long as there's good soup involved…

Scrolls of Love

Our love isn't like all those poets describe
All sonnets, and blustery prose
I've never compared thee to a summer's day
And our love's not a red, red rose.

Some days it might seem like love's not there at all
As we silently scroll through a screen
Too exhausted to chat, sat at opposite ends
With a canyon of distance between.

But… our love's a hot kettle when I make you a brew
Or you knowing which week for green bins
Our love sounds like "Hey Tesco had your favourite soup
So I've bought you a couple of tins!"

Our love sounds like sighs at the end of a day
When our babies are snugly in bed
It sounds like the text saying **Hey, got here safe!**
So you know I'm not missing or dead.

It sounds like the words to that weird random song
And that joke others don't understand
Or the way that you'll see a dead dad on TV
And instinctively reach for my hand.

It looks like the furious text I'll type out,
Then delete – as my words seem too stern
But sometimes I send it, and often you laugh
As you quell my contempt with concern.

You're the chamomile tea to my caffeine
You're the Mulligan to my O'Hare
And as I've just said – we ain't Shakespeare
But like a summer's day – we are rare!

Why is it that these days we're expected to pick a side on everything? And we can't just be agnostic or even be able to see both sides because social media encourages us to go to war with each other over ridiculous things like if we like/dislike a celebrity. Being on the fence isn't acceptable – it seems we simply have to stand fully for something, otherwise we're against it – even discussing the colour of a dress can descend into ridiculously heated debates that end up completely off topic and getting personal. This poem is a parody of how debates on social media over innocuous things often end up playing out...

Marmite

I love it.
I have it every day on toast
Of all of the spreads, it's the one I love most.

I hate it.
It's awful stuff, all gooey and icky
And I can't stand the way that it makes your knife sticky.

Well, I love it.
Have you ever had it with melted cheese?
Everyone who's tried it on crumpets agrees.

I hate it.
Don't tell me I should enjoy the stuff.
I tried it ONCE and that was ENOUGH!

Just saying that I love it
I'm not sure why you're starting to shout
You're clearly the one who's missing out.

Well, I've already said – I HATE it
All I can say is you deserve all the flak
If you can eat something so tar-like and black

Don't try to tell me what I should eat
You're just jealous and bitter that you're missing a treat

Where did I say that? Stop overreacting!
If you were here in person you'd get your face smacked in!

Ha! Just looked at your profile, what an ugly mug!
Hardly surprising you act like a thug!

People like you PISS ME OFF – keyboard warrior!
If you was here now you'd be the one who was sorrier!

Oh, you think you're so hard, threatening people online
Go and grow some balls, while you're there – grow a spine!

I've got a spine thanks, and a MASSIVE ball bag,
And I've better things to do than sit rowing with a slag.

Yeah, well BYE THEN! (inserts emoji of waving hand)
I've reported your comments, so enjoy being banned!

*That very last comment went completely unread
Once he'd called her a slag, he just left the whole thread.*

Now two separate people go two separate ways.
Now there's two angry starts to two angry days.
And the burning issue that brought things to a head?
A slight disagreement over yeast-based spread!

You see, this is the internet, so in this modern day.
There's no middle ground, and no such shade as grey.
You must make your decision – Is it black? Is it white?
Do you love it? Or hate it? It's important, Marmite!

(PS I know "sorrier" isn't a word, but people who argue on social media with strangers don't care about stuff like that!)

Chapter Three: I Can Hear You Lying

Why Politics is All Bollocks

Whilst reading some comments about the coronation of King Charles on social media, the discussion turned to the topic of how children at the local primary school were marking the occasion. When one user mentioned that her daughter's school weren't doing anything, the discussion exploded into a flurry of outlandish, unfounded nonsense.

Much of this was instigated by a red-faced man called Gary who was holding a carp in his profile picture, and who essentially used the discussion to spout his own hateful agenda. This inspired the below poem, as I could just imagine Gary sat in a pub, nursing a pint, and moaning to his mates about the fact he's not allowed to smoke indoors anymore...

The Gammon's Lament

You can't have Easter, you can't have eggs
You can't tell the waitress that she's got nice legs
You can't make jokes about gypsies selling pegs
This island has become a bore!

It upsets the disabled, the word "walkie talkie"
And don't dare say coloured, or darkie, or chalky
The Jews get offended if you say the word "porky"
You can't say anything anymore!

It's St Georges Day, but my kids can't wear their finery
Coz it "offends all the Muslims" at Gatley Primary
I'd complain to the teacher, but I'm told SHE'S non-binary
And the head's name is Mrs Kapoor!

And don't get me started on everyone's gender
Identifying as a woman? Just a sex offender
In my day you simply just called them a bender
But you can't say anything anymore!

Please don't shut down Clarkson, he says it how it is
And yes, I mean HE as in He, Him, and His
And if you're unmarried you're a Miss or a Ms
Be grateful you're not called a whore!

And it's like that Sam Smith, it's just all for attention
HIS attempt to be different, to defy all convention
But say that out loud and it just causes tension
You can't say anything anymore!

ALL lives matter, never mind just the blacks
What about all us whites who get racial attacks?
It's just a doll on a jam jar – so why all the flak?
You can't say anything anymore!

They don't want to hear it, this snowflake generation
They're happy to deny the demise of our nation
Oooh I've committed a crime – I'm a straight male Caucasian
That's enough to see me wrestled to the floor

They come over on boats, the whole thing's gone to shit
I'm not being racist, I'm just a patriotic Brit
But dare say that you're proud to be English - that's it!
I've worked hard all my life, and what for?

Getting options to read my next gas bill in Urdu?
Getting SARS, Swine flu, Covid, Ebola, or Bird Flu?
Ever felt like you've ranted but nobody's heard you?
You can't say anything anymore!

*I was inspired to write this after I read an article in the
newspaper about how social services are less likely to follow
up and act on concerns over child protection if the family
happen to be that "magic combination" of white and middle
class. You only have to look at how we view things so very
differently depending on the social status of the parents. If we
saw a school mum sat in the garden of her council house
drinking at lunchtime, we have a tendency to view this
unfavourably. Yet swap out council mum for middle-class
mum, move the setting to a boutique bistro, and suddenly
we're making "mummy wine time" jokes and displaying
plaques in the kitchen like "Gin & Tonic – Mummy's Little
Helper!"*

*This poem looks at some of the privileges that the wealthier
in society hold, and is an (imaginary) conversation between
two social workers...*

Tesco Value White

Did you see all the beer cans lined up on the shelf? The bottle bin
heavier than her soul itself?
Did you think that this woman appeared in good health? As I'm not
quite sure what I should write.

*But the cans were craft ale and belonged to her fella – an established
surveyor. They've got a wine cellar!
It's not like they were cans of White Lightning, or Stella. I think that
it's probably alright.*

Did you hear how she spoke though? Of feeling unable? How the
life she once had felt no more than a fable?
And I'm sure I saw sleeping pills on her hall table, do you think that
they're just used at night?

Well, we all know it's hard for these middle-class mothers,
they've built their career and when kids come, that suffers.
Her handbag was expensive – she's not like the others. I think that
it's probably alright.

Did you not think it odd that she talked oh so quickly? She couldn't
meet our gaze, and her toddler looked sickly.
And she sniffed all the time, and her nose was quite trickly. And have
you ever seen her eat a bite?

It's not like we saw powder all clogged round her nose, it's just that
time of year – hay fever I suppose.
She's just trapped in a life that she never quite chose, but I reckon
it's probably alright.

But I went near the toddler, he actively flinched. With those marks
on his forearm – do you think he'd been pinched?
I know if we're wrong here we're gonna get lynched – but something
just doesn't feel right.

Oh, show me one kid who's not a bit nervous, she answered all our
questions, her manner impervious
It's just a nice, normal couple who really don't deserve us turning
up at their house in the night.

Do you read the local paper? Or do you usually bin it?
Guess who got in her Audi with that toddler strapped in it?
And the coroner's report stated OVER THE LIMIT
And the signs all along shone a light.

Well, our service is stretched and we know, for that matter, rich AND
poor folk fail but it's usually the latter,
I looked in her bread bin, they had Waitrose ciabatta, not Tesco
Value White.

Inspired by Brian Bilston's wonderful poem "How Much I Dislike the Daily Mail" it got me thinking about the puerile (but very funny) game of "Would You Rather" that we used to play on nights out. Somehow that evolved into odious politicians because I guess that's just how my brain works!

Taking the "Would You Rather" Game to the Extreme

Would you rather…

1. Lick the puckered anus of a rabid dog?
2. Run your finger round the rim of a public bog?
3. Watch a tramp throw up and then ask him for a snog?
4. Drive over Snake's Pass in thick winter fog?
5. Sit down and study Piers Morgan's blog?
6. Get kicked in the fanny by a wooden clog?
7. Place your tongue on the back of a Poison Dart frog?
8. Buy some overpriced trainers from the Freemans catalogue?
9. Deliberately trap your tit in a steam engine's cog?

'Coz while this list of atrocities may leave you agog,

I would rather do all of them, than do Jacob Rees-Mogg!

Get out your pizza cutter and sing along to the tune of That's Amore! Huge apologies to Dean Martin, or anyone who previously enjoyed this song and now cannot decouple it from these lyrics!

That's a Tory

When you're devoid of hope, but you're told you should cope
That's a Tory.

When your lifestyle is bashed, as your incomes are slashed
That's a Tory.

On the dole, renting out a hole, ownership a goal so you self-soothe with Stella.
Get shit pay, told that it's OK, living every day like a Dickens novella.

When the posh private schools, churn out 'out of touch' fools
That's a Tory.

When the mum down the street can't buy clothing or heat – you're not shocked.

When some pensioners die, and it's lie after lie – fuck the poor, eh?

Plain to see, on the BBC, Hunt and Cleverley, sure that you'll agree
That's a Tory!

One weekend in November, when my well of inspiration had dried up, I asked my social media community to suggest some poetry topics and committed to choosing one at random and writing about it. The suggestions ranged from the sublime to the ridiculous as you can probably imagine, but none so ridiculous as this one that got selected and was suggested by my friend Dave Bryden!

So once again, thank you Dave for everything. It's been character building....

For this poem, I imagined what might happen if a normal, cheap camping chair had magical powers, and it turned anyone who sat in it into a racist...

The Racist Chair

As we go through life, I think that it's nice
To pass along wisdom, and helpful advice
I like to think that it sometimes makes
The recipient dodge the same mistakes.

This isn't somewhere that you'll find
Trite quotes like "Follow your dreams!" "Be kind!"
The cautionary tale I'd like to share
Is - *Never sit in the racist chair!*

The racist chair was built by mystics
Then by transcendental, strange logistics
Bypassed the matrix, and hit the stores
More precisely, Stockport's *Go Outdoors*.

It is said that he who takes the seat
Will feel an immediate urge to Tweet
About migrant kids on the Dover coast,
Before sharing a Katie Hopkins post.

His face will get redder, his belly fatter,
He'll involuntarily bellow "All Lives Matter!"
A crowd will gather, and stare on, perplexed
At some of the things that happen next.

He's still in the chair, and he grips the arms firmly
And declares his intention to drive to Burnley
To join in a rally led by Hearts of Oak
Coz "you can't say you're English these days, it's a joke"

His friends try and help him, they urge him to stand,
But he can't, and he roars "DON'T LET POPPIES GET BANNED!"
Then he goes on a rant about terror attacks
That seems woefully absent of tangible facts.

But that doesn't stop him, it doesn't end there
For he can't break the spell of the racist chair
He won't listen to logic, or a sane point of view
He gets HIS facts from Facebook, so he KNOWS they are true.

There's just one surefire way to undo this chair curse
And you need to act quickly, before things get worse
You simply shout "Look! There are some Christmas ads!"
"Those families are Asian! And one has two dads!"

And the shock and the outrage from this indignation
Will make him leap up from sheer exasperation!
And the spell will be lifted, the voodoo ends there
And back into the void goes the racist chair.

What became of the chair? Where did it go next?
No one's really sure, but they say it's still hexed.
Some think it's in Kent, home of prejudiced Boomers.
Some say Boris has got it, but of course…they're just rumours!

When I was made redundant, I decided that there'd be no harm in applying for Jobseekers Allowance while I looked for a job because I'd paid in all my life, right? Unfortunately, because I had a little part-time evening job (6 hours a week) the very helpful people at the DWP decided that I was entitled to the grand total of £1.23 a week, which was almost worse than if they'd offered me fuck all! I was very lucky because my husband was working, so we weren't desperate, but it just shows how out of touch the government are if they actually think that offering someone £1.23 a week to live on is acceptable, given how much things – not luxury items – but necessities now cost.

This all happened in the same week that Prime Minister Rishi Sunak told us all just to buy cheaper bread, and Suella Braverman declared being homeless a "lifestyle choice" which was a real treat. There's nothing like being told how to budget by millionaires, eh?!

*Anyhow, it got me thinking about the current cost of living, and all the things that you **can't** buy with £1.23…*

My Favourite Things

Tissues for noses, or cat food for kittens
A raincoat that closes, or warm woollen mittens
A small Lidl food shop, a late payment fee
These can't be paid for with one twenty-three.

New shoes and trousers that don't have big holes in
Basic school notebooks - not fancy, or moleskin
A pen that might last through that GCSE
All out of reach with my one twenty-three.

Asda brand trainers, not flash or designer.
Sanitary towels for my bleeding vagina
A pint of cow's milk to make warm cups of tea
Nope – not for you, you've got one twenty-three.

When the cold bites
When the rent's due
When I'm feeling sad
I simply take Rishi's advice about bread
And then I don't feel so bad!

Bus fare to work, or a card for the meter
A pack of beef mince, or an hour with the heater
An eye test and glasses, so that I can see
These are beyond my one pound twenty-three.

Cheap Christmas stockings, with felt tips and socks in
A calendar to open with pictures and chocs in
Turkey, or crackers, or even a tree
No Christmas for those who have one twenty-three.

When I can't cope
When the kids cry
When I'm going mad
I remember that this
is "my lifestyle
choice"
And then I don't feel
so bad!

Chapter Four: I Can Hear You Adulting

Adulting – Zero Stars. Do Not Recommend

*Those freebie/giveaway sites on Facebook are the most
bizarre thing sometimes, as it's surprising the shite that
people will take off your hands (a bag of used bottle tops and
a three-legged chair is the most bizarre thing I've seen get
snapped up!)*

*This poem was inspired by my most recent attempt to give
away my old Dyson vacuum cleaner on a local give-away
site. Why are people such time wasters?!*

Can I Be Considered, Please?

I was giving away a hoover, to be fair – a solid deal!
A little old but cherished, if you ignore the squeaky wheel
Too good to resign to the local tip, or to Facebook Marketplace
I stuck it on a "freebie" site so it wouldn't go to waste.

It's the first time that I'd done this, I did NOT expect to face
The exasperating idiots that infiltrate this space!
"Wud luv dis pls" said Kyle, five secs after I'd posted.
He seemed quite keen, so I didn't think all my texts would then be
ghosted!

Next in line was Dylan, Kyle's interest now dismissed…
But Dylan didn't want it, he'd just commented when pissed!
It stated *please collect today* and on that, I was quite clear.
Was I naïve to assume that all responders would live near?

In comes Carol with a comment, stating she would love to take it
If she finished work and came straight here, she was confident she'd
make it.
But alas, when bedtime rolled around, no Carol was in sight.
I'd had no WhatsApps, calls or texts – so I turned in for the night.

The next day I had "Sorry luv – just couldn't get to you!
Is there a chance that you'd deliver? I'm about a mile or two!"
It's not ideal but I wanted rid;
"Where to?" I asked quite sternly.
Well noting I'm in Sale…. Carol lives in fucking BURNLEY!

"No sorry that's too far" I said – remember, this is free?!
"When you factor in the petrol, this will end up costing *me*!"
"Well, this is for my daughter, she's just going through a divorce"
I'm not sure how that's relevant… and do I look like Parcelforce?!

Oh, WHY is this so difficult? I do NOT want a fee!
And let me say this once again – the bastard thing is FREE!
That's when I got the hammer, unleashed all my rage and wrath.
"NO ONE GETS IT NOW!" I laughed, as the police carted me off.

My psychiatrist looks at me, taps her pen in deft manoeuvre
"So, you say your issues started when you gave away a hoover?"
I take one pill each morning now, they keep my mind robust.
Oh, RIP dear hoover, you live no more to gather dust.

I first wrote this poem in my head, on a tram into the city centre one typical rainy day, when I knew that I'd be getting soaked the minute I got off. I wondered what Rudyard Kipling (the original creator of this iconic poem that I've shamelessly borrowed from) would make of my beloved city that I've been lucky enough to call home for over 40 years.

If

If you can look at a sandwich and call it a "barm"
And call the accompanying tea "a brew"
If you know to keep your wits about you, to avoid harm
In Piccadilly Gardens, at half past two.

If you can wait, and prepare to never go far
On matchday trams, full up to the brim
Or not much mind the sticky floors of Dry Bar
When so many others would deem it grim.

If you can dream of a deserted Albert Square
Where rows of taxis queue to take you home
Or think fondly of Fifth Avenue whilst you're there
With its 50p drinks and its foam.

If you can stare up at an illuminated Town Hall Santa
As the season gets wetter, and even colder
Or try and blag your way into Press Club with banter
Whilst trying and hoping to look much older.

If you can scale the stone steps of Afflecks
And confidently know the way to Deansgate Locks
And feel strange pride at the mention of legends
Joy Division, Oasis, Buzzcocks.

If you can't stomach dry chips in London town
Knowing that gravy is what's required
Or stay until the bitter end in Jilly's Rock World, coming down
And not ever admit to being tired.

If you can watch your lifelong team get beat
In the derby, and yet remain sanguine
If the endless rain can seep through your trainers and soak your feet
And you can simply say it's 'angin.

If you can stare, at dusk, at John Rylands Library
And watch its shadow in the setting sun
Yours is the city and everything that's in it.
And – which is more – you'll be a Manc, my son.

Oh, how I wish I knew then what I know now.

Nothing against Zoe Ball personally by the way, I suspect that she was another victim of a media that portrayed her in a certain light that she then had to try and live up to.

PS I knew, somewhere within myself when I started this poetry project, that I'd manage to shoehorn the topic of fingering in somewhere!

A Letter to My Younger Self... in the 90's

Dear Kate,

You're young and you're daft, and you probably need
Some clear words of wisdom, so please do take heed
I'm much older now (not far off forty-three!)
So here's some advice to the young you, from me...

Let's start with the lad mags that are such a big deal,
Those models are airbrushed, and none of it's real
So what if you don't look like *that* in the nude?
They're all written by men who'd prefer you subdued.

Be proud of your features, embrace how you look
Coz three decades from now you will NOT give a fuck
Your tits are fantastic - these are their best years!
Honey, once you've fed kids, they'll be like Spaniel's ears!

And fuck ladette culture, and fuck Zoe Ball
You don't need to aspire to "having it all"
You don't need to give blow jobs to boys to be cool
Or get fingered by bum-fluff-faced wankers in school.

Aim to be more than a hot High Street Honey
Oh, and Kickers as school shoes? Shit value for money!
If you're doing fake tan, please girl, moisturise first
Coz that "bright orange ankle" look is just the worst!

Be there for your girls, you're all in this together
Don't shag boys who have girlfriends, it's not big or clever
There'll be no greater songs than the ones from this era
Try and save a deposit, coz houses get dearer!

Just coz you've had sex, doesn't mean you're a slag
If a boy says it does – that's a MASSIVE red flag!
If you're ever dubbed "dick-tease" say "thanks very much"
And run – coz your body is just *yours* to touch.

Dream Matte Mousse foundation is not your best friend
If you just wait a decade, you'll be taught how to blend!
Blistering jelly shoes are replaced by FitFlops
Jane Norman and Kookai will vanish from shops.

You'll forge your own journey, you'll exert your choice
Men will try to derail you, and silence your voice
Like those hands that creep north in your grey NAF NAF sweater
It's upwards. And I promise you babe – things get better.

6th November is National Nacho Day! Who knew eh? No major meaning or thought went into this poem if I'm honest, but I bloody love nachos!

Happy Nacho Day

Much more than the humble Dorito
And as Mexican as Andres Garcia
Far crunchier than a burrito
With more bite than your standard tortilla

They're eaten at every sports ground
With hot melted Monterey Jack
They can be triangular OR round
They are nacho average snack!

When I started to look for jobs again, I dipped my toe back into the world of LinkedIn and trawling through job adverts, and it occurred to me just how much "job-speak" exists out there. I ended up finding the whole thing so corporate and soulless that I closed the website and wrote a poem about it instead...

Open to Work

Create the perfect CV!
Upgrade your resume!
Make sure employers hire YOU!
That's what the adverts say.

For the last two years, my two main skills
Have been arse-wiping and lactation.
Perhaps a look on LinkedIn will provide some inspiration?

And now I feel despondent, disconcerted, in a fluster
As I read the corporate bullshit that I'm going to have to muster.

Here's a puzzle: why the need
To state that I am "driven?"
As opposed to what? A lazy git?
Surely it's a given?

I have to use words like *delivered* when in fact I just mean *done*
I have to say *parental role* instead of *full-time mum*
And if I don't use phrases like "high pressure's where I thrive"
They'll assume that I'm a slacker, who'll slope off at ten to five.

I'm "seeking a new challenge" not just "looking for a job"
And "I share authentic viewpoints" means "I've got a massive gob"
One interview won't be enough, I'm told it's "multi-stage"
And I can't just simply chat to folk. Oh no, I must "engage"

And, if someone wants to talk, then they in turn "reach out"
(Which is better than my toddler, if I'm needed, he'll just shout!)
The weirdest phrase I've found so far is "top down" – just bizarre!
I've done that for the last two years, in a milky nursing bra.

I'm advised that all these buzzwords help to "boss" my interview
But if I stroll in and "be a boss" how will we know who's who?!
I want a job where I can just be me, no nonsense, crap, or fluff,
A job where plain old normal words are deemed to be enough.

No bullshit bingo, corporate lingo, tautology, or hype
Perhaps it's time to just accept I'm not the corporate type.

There's been a spate of awful accidents in the news recently, involving young people either stealing cars or bikes, or driving them irresponsibly. In some cases, they've collided with other vehicles, sadly losing their lives in the process. It's interesting how the media reports on these stories, and some of the language they use in the articles. Whilst there's no doubt who is at fault for the accident, the fact they've died seems to absolve them of any wrongdoing in the eyes of the media.

This then results in an outpouring of grief on social media too, as tributes pour in from people who knew them – which proves very divisive. If anyone dares point out that the deceased was in the wrong, they are frequently set upon and attacked for their opinion.

Yes, the loss of life is indeed tragic, but it's also completely preventable.

Heart of Gold

A cheeky, bright, courageous boy
Known by all on the estate
Just a kid obsessed with motorbikes
Dean didn't deserve this fate

Loved by everyone he met
His laughter filled the room
He'll fly high with the angels now
God took him way too soon

He was just mucking around that night
When he broke in and nicked them keys
Not like there was kids in the house
So can we show some respect, please?

The bike was probably insured
And how can anyone be cross?
What about his mum? Her baby's gone
She's suffered the biggest loss

And the family in the car he hit?
At least they're still alive
What about our Dean? Our blue-eyed boy?
He's the one who didn't survive!

Don't talk to me about mental scars
How can that driver claim
That the image will haunt him forever?
It's like he's saying Dean's to blame!

The newspaper's calling it tragic
But the comments on Facebook are cruel
There's just no need for his family to read
"What a selfish and reckless young fool"

I'm off to lay flowers there later
And there's fireworks from midnight 'til three
Forever in our hearts, Saint Dean of the estate
Til we meet again bro, RIP

I originally wrote 'Mind the Gap' ahead of International Men's Day, as I was thinking about the language we use around children and how the vast difference in how we speak to them can shape their perceptions of their own capabilities.

Numerous studies have shown that gender stereotyping starts really early on in childhood. I vividly recall being in primary school and a teacher coming in asking for "two big strong boys" to help complete a physical task! We also tend to praise attributes of strength and intellect in young boys and focus more on appearance for girls – "oh what a pretty dress" and so forth.

Studies also estimate that women will only apply for a role if they fit the criteria 100% whereas men will apply with a 60% skills match.

The language we use around young children is so important...

Mind the Gap

What are little boys made of?
Slugs and snails and puppy dog's tails
Given advice to "man up" if he ails
Advocacy and easement to conquer pay scales
(Three quarters of worldwide CEOs are males)
That's what little boys are made of.

What are little girls made of?
Sugar and spice and all things nice
Boardroom or baby? Choose. Sacrifice
The same expertise but at half the price
7% gender pay gap? Yeah, that should suffice
That's what little girls are made of.

I started thinking about all the things that make Northerners Northern, and decided that if I was going to write something on that topic, it'd probably need an entire book of its own!

However, one thing stuck out to me distinctly. I remember ordering a full English breakfast in London a few years back, and the beans were not on the toast, or even on the plate, but in a little ramekin dish on the side. When I spoke of this atrocity to my Northern friends, their level of shock and outrage was palpable, hence I thought this was a good starting point...

The Importance of Bean Northern

I'm convinced that being Northern means
Getting very precious about baked beans
So, when a café breakfast's ordered (fried)
Those beans must NOT be on the side!

Oh mate, you'll lose that tip so fast
(As has genuinely happened in the past)
If you try and be all upmarket and swish
And you put my beans in a little dish.

Beans have no place on the wing
They're not a spare part, or an optional thing
Those who do this have neglected, I feel
To honour their significance in the meal.

So, bollocks to hipster cafes in Brixton
Me? I'd rather eat in Flixton
Where cafés know what matters most
And those beans go on top of (buttered) toast.

My sister Marie is terrified of birds of prey, which is unfortunate as she lives in Qatar where many of the Qatari men own falcons and travel around with them. They also bring them on commercial flights to the UK which has made for some interesting tales when she's been travelling back to the UK and had to change seats due to being seated next to a random falcon!

I recently found out that to fly to the UK, these falcons need passports, which sent me off down an internet rabbit hole looking at falcon passports. I was disappointed to learn that they don't need photos in their little falcon passport, as I quite liked the idea of falcons smoothing their feathers and cramming into a photo booth in Max Spielman trying to capture the perfect picture!

Anyway – I wrote this when I'd been woken up by a toddler at 3am and I really should've just been sleeping...but welcome to the inside of my head and be thankful you don't live in it!

Love Birds

She may have had an impressive wingspan
But this would be her first long-haul flight
They'd met weeks before on *Peregrindr*
(A bird of prey matchmaking site)

He'd invited her over to Qatar
That Sheikh, with a yacht in Al-Khor
He assured her that he was a gentleman
He seemed nice – but her friends were unsure.

He's giving you the fly-around said Buzzard,
I'll bet he's got a Red Kite at home!
You'll have to pick up the pieces and carrion, warned Vulture
When you're set loose in Qatar alone!

Admittedly, there'd been a few red flags
Like their video chat just last week
When she'd spotted a gauntlet on his bedside drawer
Or those texts – SEND ME PICS OF UR BEAK!

But it was years since she'd felt this happy
They'd found each other – two lonely souls
And she could leave behind the harsh countryside winter
No more hunting for field mice and voles.

So here she sits, in a Boots photo booth
And she daydreams of those airport gates
The camera flashes, there's no turning back
The flight path to true love awaits.

74

I threw myself into the new year with a whole heap of weird symptoms, and I realised how furious my body probably was with me. There it is, trying its best to become perimenopausal and I'm confusing the hell out of it by continuing to breastfeed a toddler. I think my hormones (and boobs) are ready for a rest now, but my boss is incredibly unreasonable. Shouts, claws at my top, and sometimes throws toys if I refuse his requests. I wish I had a HR department.

I feel for my ovaries, I really do. I suspect this is what it's like when you've planned a nice retirement and then find out you must work for a further five years. I bet they're fuming. No wonder they went and sought some legal advice...

Legal Representation

Dear Mrs Hook

Allow me to introduce myself and explain why I write.
I represent your ovaries, and seek assistance with their plight
The main concern my clients raise is their unmet expectation
Heading towards retirement, they had planned some relaxation.

They've served you well for many years, as you'll agree no doubt
And they rather hoped by now there'd be less oestrogen about.
But you chose to child bear late in life, and you then assumed a need
To "organically parent" for two years, namely – breastfeed.

And whilst producing milk, and whilst your toddler's having suction
Your ovaries have borne the brunt of this hormone production
My clients feel confused by this, you've gone against the grain
So I write to ask you clearly if from feeding, you'll refrain.

That would allow my clients to desist from their main chores
And gracefully retire into perimenopause.

They simply ask for respite, so instead of monthly eggs
They perform their duties quarterly and rest their weary legs
And when they feel this is too much, their duties will decrease
Perhaps to once or twice a year, and eventually – they'll cease.

I appreciate that this request may seem to you obscure
But if I may, I'll put this to you with a metaphor
Imagine booking a Saga cruise, to somewhere quiet and warm
But on getting off the plane you find The Strip in Benidorm!

My clients state they've pushed out eggs since you were just thirteen
"If we wanted to get screwed" they said, "We'd have worked for
Philip Green!"
So I ask that you take note, and begin the weaning stage
And allow your ovaries to retire, into graceful older age.

Your Sincerely

A. Solicitor

Chapter Five: I Can Hear You Drinking

Christmas – Different Year, Same Bollocks

At the risk of sounding like a miserable cow, I find the whole annual debacle of putting up the Christmas tree so angst-ridden. There's always a drama. This year, I put it up to find that the stump was wonky so I couldn't get it to stand properly without leaning, and my ageing cats also enjoy pissing up the side of it. And that's even before the toddler has tried to climb it...

O Christmas Tree

O Christmas tree, O Christmas tree,
How stressful is your presence?
O Christmas tree, O Christmas tree,
I need anti-depressants.

Not only do you shed your pines,
But you're a loo for our felines,
O Christmas tree, O Christmas tree,
How flaky are your branches?

O Christmas tree, O Christmas tree,
Quite bare you could be lovely,
O Christmas tree, O Christmas tree,
My kids have made you ugly.

Each year you're draped in gaudy light,
Adorned with school and nursery shite,
O Christmas tree, O Christmas tree,
You're fuelling my anxiety.

The festive season can be incredibly difficult for many, but perhaps none more so than those people in their forties who are lactose intolerant....

(Sing to the tune of "Galveston" by Glen Campbell)

Gaviscon

Gaviscon, oh Gaviscon, I can feel my acid flowin'
And there's no escapin' knowin'
By half past one, I'll need you, Gaviscon.

Gaviscon, oh Gaviscon, while the cheese and wine were smashin'
To the spoon drawer I'll be dashin'
Take the biggest one, and pour out Gaviscon.

I know I shoulda stuck to drinkin' water
Instead of knockin' back that Pinos Gris
And did I really need that Brie?
Now the heartburn's the price for fun.

Gaviscon, oh Gaviscon, I feel like I am surely dyin'
And my stomach has me cryin'
This is my fifth spoonful, oh what have I become?
Oh Gaviscon, Oh Gaviscon.

In 2021 I gave birth to my son in a hospital bed, with nobody but the on-duty midwife by my side. This is because my husband and eldest son both had Covid at the time and were in the last day of their ten-day isolation period. The rules at the time meant my husband couldn't be by my side.

This honestly isn't a moan because I know so many people suffered dreadful losses as a result of Covid, but the whole thing was made even more infuriating when we found out about the festive gatherings in Downing Street and all the rule-breaking that went on there. Maybe if my child had been fathered by Boris, I would've been able to bend the rules?!

Anyway – 2021 was the start of a lovely little festive family tradition where one of us (usually my husband) gets Covid every Christmas without fail, wrecking any plans we've made…

It'll Be Covid This Christmas

Try to imagine, a table all laid
Try to imagine those plans that we made
You suggested, that I tested
There's a double red line
So I'm stuck home, and I'm all alone
Got no turkey, or red wine

It'll be Covid this Christmas
Not just a cold
It'll be Covid this Christmas
Just watch it unfold
This is getting old, so old, can't mix my household
This Christmas

It's giving me flashbacks, of Boris's stupid face
And how we would listen to the rules he put in place
But I pour a drink, and I have a think
About reasons we can meet
Like for cheese and wine, and for party time
Like they did in Downing Street

It'll be Covid this Christmas
Not just a cold
It'll be Covid this Christmas
Just watch it unfold
This is getting old, so old, can't mix my household
This Christmas.

Merry Christmas Boris.... Wherever you are!

Why oh why did I try and brave the Trafford Centre a week before Christmas? I never learn! People absolutely lose all sensibilities at this time of year though, so it's hardly a surprise that festive shopping lends itself to outrage and annoyance. As I fought my way through crowds, sweating and furious under my layers, unable to muster an ounce of patience, I heard this festive classic and decided to re-jig it...

Wanker Wonderland

Car horns blare, no one's listening.
Tempers flare, spouses bristling.
A too common sight
We might see a fight
Shopping in a wanker wonderland.

Some old cow, with a po-face
Saunters round, at a slow pace
Then in front of me
She stops suddenly
Shopping in a wanker wonderland.

In each window I can see a Santa
And I remind myself why I am here
Someone trips me up, I mutter *wanker*
And vow to do it all online next year!

Need to sit, been stood ages
Benches draped in teenagers
I just want some space
Get out of my face
Shopping in a wanker wonderland

Feeling stressed, I try to grab a coffee
Although I've not exactly got the time
It's rammed, and I can't get a seat for toffee
Fuck this shit, I'm ordering off Prime…

I've got nothing I went for
Fuck knows who this was meant for
But I'll take the flak
As I'm NOT going back

Shopping in a wanker wonderland
Shopping in a wanker wonderland

The local Facebook group for my area doesn't half provide some fantastic material from the things people post. I've checked with friends and family who live in other areas and by all accounts, the same themes crop up regardless of which area people live in.

I tried to capture all the shite that people moan about in this poem. Apart from the debates about dog poo, as I wrote this a few days before Christmas and dog poo just isn't very festive!

Your Neighbourhood Facebook Group at Christmas

Oh, the weather outside is bobbins
We've got far more pigeons than robins
The helicopter's out again
Let it rain, let it rain, let it rain!

Someone's wound up about parking
Someone's angry coz dogs are barking
Is Washway Road down to one lane?
Let it rain, let it rain…

When you find a bank card in the street
You're just trying to stop its misuse
So you blank the name, being discreet
Then you post it and get pure abuse!

There are CAPITALS meaning YELLING!
And some rather dubious spelling
Anonymous posts cause disdain
Let it rain, let it rain, let it rain!

Sometimes we are helpful and nice
As we warn of cold-callers or thieves
But this month, our bin's been nicked twice
And we're moaning at drains blocked with leaves!

There are youths on quad bikes rampaging
And the "fireworks debate" is raging
New Year's Eve will kick it all off again
Let it rain, let it rain, let it rain!

There's so much pressure at new year to try and hope for some kind of improved version of yourself, and I know that when I've made resolutions in the past, I've set such lofty goals that I've given up by day three and I'm back on the chocolate digestives. So, hats off to anyone who makes them, sticks to them, gets some joy from working towards them and all that lovely stuff. But I've pretty much given up on myself now...

New Year's Resolutions

I don't want to starve to drop post-Christmas pounds
I don't want McDonalds to be out of bounds
I don't want to juice, or drink rancid green shakes
Or make the kind of grand gestures that everyone makes.

I don't want to try a new hobby, or sport
Or to run around walloping balls on a court
I'm not joining a gym, it'll be bloody chokka
Or doing RED January, unless R means Rioja.

I won't be learning a language, conquering hills
Paying off my overdraft, or learning new skills
You won't find me bingeing on trite self-help books.
Nah – I've one resolution – to give fewer fucks!

Acknowledgements

The writing bit has been the easy (and enjoyable) bit of this book, it's been everything else in the publishing process that's been crazy. What a minefield it is getting your sweary little rhymes into print – who knew eh?!

However, it's a minefield that I couldn't have navigated without help from some bloody amazing and talented people like my wonderful proofing/editing/formatting guru **Helena** who will probably block my number after this project because I was such a pain in the arse, requesting more tweaks than a Kardashian! Before she took on this project, I should've probably mentioned that I should be in some kind of locked ward.

Douglas at SPP has also been amazing and on-hand for me and fielded the most stupid of questions at all hours. Another one who'll deffo block me!

I've also had help from some legends who've trodden this path previously, like **Steven Kedie** (author of *Suburb* and *Running and Jumping* available on Amazon!) and **Jemma Munford** aka "Blissed Out Babies" who has written an incredible book *The Better Sleep Blueprint* about infant and toddler sleep. If you're sat up reading this at 3:45 am and identifying with the parenting poems, I assure you, her book is a life saver!

I'd also like to thank my incredible friends **Claire Purcell** and **Laura Johnson**, who've woken up to (or been woken up by) my 3am WhatsApp messages containing random poems. Thanks for your constant encouragement to keep going. Keep going with the writing, I mean. Not keep going with waking you up at 3am!

To every single person who's followed me on socials, liked my poems, shared my posts, and bought this book – a colossal THANK YOU from the bottom of my heart. I hope my words have brought you comfort, amusement, joy, or whatever you've needed at that moment. Once you've read it, you're welcome to pass it on to whoever you feel might also need these words. Copyright Schmopyright eh?!

To my amazing mum **Dee**, and to my brilliant **sisters**, who've been telling me since I was young that I need to start writing – I have so much love for you that I can't even find the words for it. Unusual for me, I know!

And for my incredible sister **Marie** – I couldn't help you when you were going through the hardest time of your life, so all I could do was write, in the hope that I could somehow make you better. I hope this has done you proud.

Once upon a time (when I was about six) Marie's husband **Miller** printed all my childhood poetry off and made it into a ribbon-bound book for me. That was no mean feat in the eighties I assure you, so it probably took him about a week to type it all up and print it off!
Miller - you told me that I'd one day write a poetry book and it seems you were right as bloody usual! I like to think that my first ever poem about snowdrops will one day be as valuable as an original Picasso!

Thank you also to some of the amazing poets for inspiring me – there are too many to name individually but let's try - **Pin Badges, Thick Richard, Linda Downs, Janine Reid, Dominic Berry, Leah Stone, Nelly Bryce, Amy Langley**, and finally a huge thanks to the wonderful **Sarah Pritchard** for hosting *Write Out*

Loud where I first got the bollocks to stand up and read poems, despite me getting utterly shitfaced on Malbec, to give me the confidence to get up in the first place!

Thanks to **Michelle** and all my amazing ladies in the ***B for Butterfly*** Book Club – Sale's finest drinking club with a reading habit! I pray that this book doesn't appear on our next reading list as not sure I could cope with the honest feedback. Maybe buy me some pizza to take the edge off?!

A HUGE thank you to my previous employer, for restructuring and getting rid of my role while I was on maternity leave, making me redundant and ergo giving me the opportunity to finally get my arse in gear and write. You also rejected my recent job application to come back and work for you, so thank you for saving me from myself!

To my wonderfully talented illustrator **Paul Loudon**, who I have had the absolute pleasure and privilege to work with on this book. Thank you for your breathtaking talent, your creativity, your hilarious illustrations, and for always just understanding my weirdness. And also, for not being a staunch Tory because that would've been a bit awkward, and would've also put a very different spin on some of your drawings! Anyway, Axel Scheffler had better sleep with one eye open, that's all I'm saying!

(Dear reader – if you do one thing next, please check out Paul's work at @loudon.illustrator on Insta because he's awesome!)

OK Kate, this isn't the Oscars, start wrapping up now….

This wouldn't be an acknowledgements section without a huge shout out to my long-suffering but truly wonderful husband **Christian**, who has never suggested I "get a proper job" but has instead supported me through each period of "Britney craziness" and has given me the time and space I needed to create words. Thank you for your passive-aggressive loud ironing, and for shirking some of your early parenting duties. If you hadn't, then this book would've either not existed or would've had a much duller title.

(PS – you've since redeemed yourself as you're the only person I would EVER want to do this utterly crazy parenting bollocks with!)

And last but by no means least - thank you to my amazing babies Jude, Henry, and to our tiny person who never quite made it earthside. To write, you must truly feel, and you have all made me feel everything it's possible to ever feel. I am well and truly blessed. And also, VERY fucking tired. But largely blessed.

Big love – Kate x